MAMA DOT

Fred D'Aguiar

For Andrew

with very best wishes

Fred D'Aguiar

CHATTO & WINDUS · THE HOGARTH PRESS
LONDON

Published in 1985 by
Chatto & Windus The Hogarth Press
40 William IV Street
London WC2N 4DF

British Library
Cataloguing in Publication Data
D'Aguiar, Fred
Mama Dot.I. Title
811 PR9320.9.D/

ISBN 0-7011-2957-3

Phototypeset by Rowland Phototypesetting Ltd
Printed in Great Britain by
Redwood Burn Ltd
Trowbridge, Wiltshire

ACKNOWLEDGEMENTS
Some of the poems first appeared in the following: *Artrage, Caribbean Poetry Now, City Limits, News for Babylon, Poetry Review* and *Race Today*; others were broadcast on BBC Radio Three, and BBC 2.

CONTENTS

GLOSSARY

Most of the dialect words can be understood by saying them aloud, therefore only some are explained. The meaning of a few words varies according to the context of their use. In such cases both senses are included here.

bap – a surprise move
cawn – can't
deh – there, be
doan – don't
dub – reggae music with special effects
fe – to, for
gaf – have
gaff/labrish – group talk
gon – will
greenhart – a wood
gwine – going to
guinep – a fruit tree
juck – stab
jumby – a spirit
lick – beat
nah – not
Obeah – witchcraft, medicine
pan – on
rass – behind
ya – here

For my grandmothers
Hannah D'Aguiar & Edna Messiah

A Toast

Who gwine tek
we hope
gaf fe be a Midas
an rope
de sun
do wha Icarus
neva don

PART ONE Mama Dot

Mama Dot

I

Born on a sunday
in the kingdom of Ashante

Sold on monday
into slavery

Ran away on tuesday
cause she born free

Lost a foot on wednesday
when they catch she

Worked all thursday
till her head grey

Dropped on friday
where they burned she

Freed on saturday
in a new century

II

Old Mama Dot
old Mama Dot
boss a de stew-pot
she nah deal in vat
she nah bap
no style
so stop
look at Mama Dot
windin on de spot

Old Mama Dot
old Mama Dot
watch her squat
full o de nat-
-tral goodness dat
grow in de lann
she use to farm
bare hann
up evry dawn

Old Mama Dot
old Mama Dot
she nah deal wid vat-
-igan nah mek no fuss
she a deal wid duss
she swing cutlass
play big boss
lick chile rass
go to mass

Oracle Mama Dot

I am seated at her bare feet.
The rocking chair on floorboards
Of the verandah is the repeated break
Of bracken underfoot. *Where are we heading?*

Who dare speak in these moments before dark?
The firefly threads its infinite morse;
Crapauds and crickets are a mounting cacophony;
The laughter of daredevil bats.

Dusk thickens into night.
She has rocked and rocked herself to sleep.
She may hold silence for another millennium.
I see the first stars among cloud.

Angry Mama Dot

I

She gesticulates and it's sheet lightning on our world.
Our ears cannot be stopped against her raised voice.
All the crying we ever did is a roof, soaked through.
With no gaps for thought, we save the night trembling
A string of prayers in gibberish for her rage to quell.

II

The powdery collisions of moths round a lamp.
Us, out first thing, upturned face and palm.
So her peace comes. We stick close, watching.
Busy and humming with it, she throws us clean.
I am years later fighting to break my fall.

Obeah Mama Dot
(her remedies)

I

I am knotted in pain.
She measures string
From navel to each nipple.

She kneads into my belly
Driving the devil
Out of my enforced fast.

II

For the fevers to subside,
I must drink the bush
Boiled to a green alluvium,

In one headback slake;
And return to bouncing around,
Side-stepping bushes for days.

III

A head-knock mushrooms
Into a bold, bald,
Softened bulb.

Her poultice filled
At the end of a rainbow –
The sun above Kilimanjaro;

The murderous vial drawn,
Till the watery mound
Is a crater in burnt ground.

IV

Our rocking-chair counsellor:
Her words untangling us
from bramble and plimpler notions

Into this sudden miles-clearing.

Mama Dot's Food Allegory

She's in the throes of an original quarrel:
The on/off labrish of lids,
Stirred by wooden spoons
Gaffing on rims and the fire's cackle.

We'd notice our mouths
Watering: how it comes
Is like a tune in a wind
From miles hummed all day.

And every time I am amazed
To see every plate heaped
To satisfaction, knowing more
And more the workings of that first

Combine Harvester, gathering rice
In neat bales; a job she saw
To the last grain, when all we did
Was burrow in a house of hay;

Or race in paddy bags
Emptied to our fill.
We were her shoots
Sweetening with her care.

Might she have loved
The potato, dug as it is
Caked in mud, roots stubby,
Hardly knowing the sun?

So many bare-faced
Reminders of our destiny.
Sent like offerings from the dead
To pass as food, not turds.

Mama Dot's Exclusive

('Don't ask questions, you only get answers.')

She, doubled over a scrubbing-board;
His, *hide me*, hardly out before the ignorant
Stampede across the bridge at the front yard.
Her, *behind the stove*, a kiss he plants
On her parted lips in a hurry. They get
There demanding him even as her
Hands dip into the washing, ink as wet
On their search warrant; its signature
Forged with the remoteness of a jet's.

She has him breathing-in for a pleated skirt,
Trying high heels like his first steps again;
Its neat folds will disguise a rip that hurt
As he ducked through barbed wire in rain;
Its hem muddied by fields of tall grass.
Take him as drawn to an oasis of light,
This guest-house plumb in the wilderness;
Its running ad reads, *NO DISTANCE TO THE*
AIRPORT. . .
Unsure why he signed *De'ath* at the empty desk.

Having helped himself to skull-shaped keys,
He finds the bedroom like his own;
Too tired to remove make-up he was pleased
Carried him as far as the fenced zone
Their volley of shots pinged sparks off.
His head touches a blank pillowcase,
A last thought circles like a helicopter
Over a demo spilling out of a square:
How it suits like a coffin or he in her.

Mama Dot's Treatise

Mosquitoes
Are the fattest
Inhabitants
Of this republic.

They suck our blood
From the cradle
And flaunt it
Like a fat wallet.

They form dark
Haloes; we spend
Our outdoors
Dodging sainthood.

They force us
Into an all-night
Purdah of nets
Against them.

O to stop them
Milking us
Till we are bait
For worms;

Worms that don't
Know which way
To turn and will
Inherit the earth.

Mama Dot Warns Against an Easter Rising

Doan raise no kite is good friday
but is out he went out an fly it
us thinkin maybe dere wont be a breeze
strong enouf an widout any a we to hole it
fo him he'd neva manage to get it high-up
to de tree top ware de wind kissin
de ripess sweetess fruit we cawn reach
but he let out some string bit by bit
tuggin de face into de breeze
coaxin it up all de time takin a few steps back
an it did rise up bit by bit till de lang tail
din't touch de groun an we grip de palin
we head squeeze between to watch him
an trace its rise rise rise up up up in de sky
we all want to fly in like bird but can only kite
fly an he step back juss as we beginnin
to smile fo him envy him his easter risin
when bap he let out a scream leggo string
an de kite drop outta de sky like a bird
a sail down to de nex field an we runnin to him
fogetting de kite we uncle dem mek days ago
fram wood shave light as bird bone
paper tin like fedder an de tongue o kite
fo singin in de sky like a bird an de tail
fo balance string in de mout like it pullin
de longess worm an he a hole him foot
an a bawl we could a see seven inch a greenhart
gone in at de heel runnin up him leg
like a vein he groanin all de way to de haspital
on de cross-bar a bike ridden by a uncle
she not sayin a word but we hearin her
fo de ress a dat day an evry year since
doan raise no kite is good friday
an de sky was a birdless kiteless wait fo her word

Mama Dot Against the Overseas Challenge

They happen so fast, talk has it the plots rise
To meet them, out of the blue. Mama Dot said
She once saw a year's crop stripped in no time,
A radar-smell fetching them to these ripe fields;
Had shown us ways of preparing a surprise
Sure to move them on, empty-handed, if we acted
Together. It seemed we barely heard all this
Remembering the panic that clear noon-sunday.

The sky blackened this swirling drift toward us,
Thickening to a pitch as it grew close; its vermilion
Propellers filling the air. The first few resembled
The huge, dust-raising drops that start a downpour.
They smacked everyplace in the crude crash-landings
Of failed parachutes. The run for the shelter
Over their crisp, baby-haired, bullet-shapes
After some tried to pincer where they butted the flesh.

Who said she was left to them caused the scramble
Back in the open. She stood bang in their midst,
Her wide Hammer-swings beginning the Bullroarer,
Her full height partially blotted by the studio-dark
Their lowering in broad daylight directly produced.
Half landed, they dipped skywards again, our fields
Of the frail paddy-shoots that sprang from green
To an edible gold throwing them off wet-dog-like.

They drew a drilled semi-circle and marked time,
Blurting this zingy bugle, going, going, gone.
We combed the ground of each armoured trophy:
So many Mummies buried in the bottom far-corner
Of wardrobes; or impossible Houdinis balancing
Rafters, sealed in the breathless mouths of jars;
Our tongues dreading that season's care-picked rice,
Like the stay of locusts we would find hard to swallow.

Mama Dot Learns to Fly

Mama Dot watched reels of film
Of inventor after inventor trying to fly.
She's so old, she's a spectator in some.

Seeing them leap off bridges straight
Into rivers, or burn
Strapped to backfiring rockets,

Or flap about with huge wings
Only to raise a whole heap of dust,
Makes her cringe: what conviction!

How misguided. Right then, she wants
To see an ancestor, in Africa; half-way
Round the world and back through time.

Her equipment's straightforward,
Thought-up to bring the lot
To her: *Come, leh we gaff girl.*

Letter from Mama Dot

I

Your letters and parcels take longer
And longer to reach us. The authorities
Tamper with them (whoever reads this
And shouldn't, I hope jumby spit
In dem eye). We are more and more
Like another South American dictatorship,
And less and less a part of the Caribbean.
Now that we import rice (rice that used
To grow wild!), we queue for most things:
Flour, milk, sugar, barley, and fruits
You can't pick anymore. I join them
At 5 a.m. for 9 o'clock opening time,
People are stabbing one another for a place
And half the queue goes home empty-handed,
With money that means next to nothing.
Every meal is salt-fish these days; we even
Curry it. Send a box soon. Pack the basics:
Flour, for some roti; powdered milk;
And any news of what's going on here.
No luxuries please, people only talk, shoes
Can wait till things improve (dey bound
Fe improve cause dem cawn get no worse!)
Everybody fed-up in truth; since independence
This country hasn't stopped stepping back;
And if you leave you lose your birthright.
With all the talk of nationality we still hungry.
Neil has joined the forces against all advice.
He brings home sardines saved from his rations
For our sunday meal; he wears the best boots
In town. The fair is full of prizes
We threw out in better days and everyone wins
Coconuts. I wouldn't wish this on anyone,
But it's worse somehow without you here.
Write! We feast on your letters.

II

You are a traveller to them.
A West Indian working in England;
A Friday, Tonto, or Punkawallah;
Sponging off the state. Our languages
Remain pidgin, like our *dark, third,*
Underdeveloped, world. I mean, their need
To see our children cow-eyed, pot-bellied,
Grouped or alone in photos and naked,
The light darkened between their thighs.
And charity's all they give: the cheque,
Once in a blue moon (when guilt's
A private monsoon), posted to a remote
Part of the planet they can't pronounce.
They'd like to keep us there.
Not next door, your house propping-up
Theirs; your sunflowers craning over
The fence, towards a sun falling
On their side; begonias that belong
To them shouldering through its tight
Staves; the roots of both mingling.
So when they skin lips to bare teeth
At you, remember it could be a grimace
In another setting: the final sleep
More and more of us meet in our prime,
(Your New Cross fire comes to mind);
Who dream nowadays of peace.
You know England, born there, you live
To die there, roots put down once
And for all. Drop me a line soon,
You know me. *Neva see come fo see.*

Carnival Mama Dot

She stands high as the gable.
Her dreadlocks house a nothingness.
Her floorlength dress is a full sail.
She leans and earth shifts its axis,
Straight, she's the world stoodstill.
Her several hearts beat as one;
Her following dance past pain;
One appears to flaunt a flung coin –
A taunt before the lightning swoop
That has it scooped in a palm
Which never fails under her spell.

Her head at the window crowds hiding places,
Fills all space with screams;
She drowns them as she passes.
By the time we are brave enough to look,
She is seen still blotting out the sun,
Still her sound makes the ground tremble.
She leaves a hazy, shucked landscape,
Where only a humming-bird flashes from cover,
Sticks momentarily in mid-air and is gone;
Then her dust, like the impossible Atlantic-cross
Made by the Sahara, refuses to settle.

The Day Mama Dot Takes Ill

The day Mama Dot takes ill,
The continent has its first natural disaster:
Chickens fall dead on their backs,
But keep on laying rotten eggs; ducks upturn
In ponds, their webbed feet buoyed forever;
Lactating cows drown in their sour milk;
Mountain goats lose their footing on ledges
They used to skip along; crickets croak,
Frogs click, in broad daylight; fruits
Drop green from trees; coconuts kill travellers
Who rest against their longing trunks;
Bees abandon their queens to red ants,
And bury their stings in every moving thing;
And the sun sticks like the hands of a clock
At noon, drying the very milk in breasts.

Mama Dot asks for a drink to quench her feverish thirst:
It rains until the land is waist-deep in water.
She dreams of crops being lost: the water drains
In a day leaving them intact. She throws open her window
To a chorus and rumpus of animals and birds,
And the people carnival for a week. Still unsteady
On her feet, she hoes the grateful ashes
From the grate and piles the smiling logs on it.

Farewell Mama Dot

I

I'd approach unseen
Along a hair's-breadth
Perpendicular to the tsetse's
Tail, the pilot's-cockpit head
Bobbing in a coasting breeze.

Tied to string,
It circled all day
As if stacked, forgotten,
In airport cloud
And fuelled there.

Vaccines, tongue-worried
Fillings, a metal taste,
Overlapping announcements,
Crisp turnstiles,
Beginning insects at dusk.

My iron concentration
Before lassoing it,
Modelled this flight;
I piloted a cotton trail
Then, to finish seated

For five thousand miles,
On unfurling vapour.
The brittle, ornate tsetse
Stomaching better than me
A blind change of climate.

II

Her rocker halted,
Is earth's spin lost.

Her stripped bed,
Our world became savannah.

Her coffin dances down
Six feet to a wailing chorus.

Her shovelling over
Scores on greenhart, amplified;

Her ground rising-up oh Jah,
From sweet diminuendo to bass.

Her rounding off by delicate pats
With the backs of shovels.

Her new-made bed of flowers.
That second shadow *is she.*

PART TWO Roots Broadcast

Roots Broadcast

No sun nah come up
dese days yet sun muss deh
some weh shinin pan somebady
else back wen all we gat
is hevy cloud redy fe bruk
pan we head an memry
of how sun wuk cawn dead
fo dis ya roots broadcast
pickin up pickin up

Dreadtalk

'Cow neva know de use a him tail
till fly tek it.'

Who eye pass who eye
who badder dan who
who get juck who carry
blade nah fe get juck
an who lick jackass
get lix like peas
wen ass tun com roun

We all want daughta
fe fadder we chile
but daughta nah want
always absent fadder
or sweet man wid no fucha
wid no ninetofive
nor yard a credit card

An we all want custom car
fe bun-up a bit a bichemin
com sataday nite
instead a midnite pitcha
fe feed we dream wid air
is hot air we desire hot air
for de only car we drive is Tonka

An de only house we gon build
is lego de adverts no it
dem nah see we muchless talk
to we an if yu see a black
face yu see de tail end
a trend or som safety valve
move fe check anadda uprisin

So chase dem educashon
an it tun pan yu an before
yu no it yu get prosessed
brite as dem peas in a can
de britess green dat mek
yu tun-up yu nose at de
real ting it so dull

An it cawn really com
outta pod it muss be spaghetti
dem can mek yu beleave grow
pan tree or money plentiful
to be bandeed aroun wortless
dan de energy it tek fe eat
lettuce leaf an so dem tink

De folds a we brain is cabbage
pan legs only good fo runnin
roun track like jackass or dancin
pan de spat till we drap
yu cawn show me a black
who get to de tap or who nah tek
culcha pan a plate or slate

Anadda new category 'black-british'
a progeny alang a line we battle
thru a gauntlet we a run
an we tekin it up evry time
like we a see carrot but no
stick like we foget de whip
we flick a lick back a brodda

An sista who nah want pickney
she cawn feed juss fe bolsta
brodda ego she nah want revolushonary
role he a hann she so dem a cuss
wan anadda an de table den a get roun
is a lang way aff if eva an dem
only meet in a posse wid a soun

Far is rave dem want fe rave
com sataday nite an de blues
dem a keep at arms length is de bady
dem a rub-up in a heavy dub stile
it safa dan blade an de adda
blue dat a krawl roun in packs
fe pounce pan we in braad daylite

An it betta dan gettin lack-up
in a ward ware yu cawn let aff
steem widout de vial dem a pump
in yu vane dat a beet out
yu brain till yu feel like fish
outta yu debt in a blue
deepa dan eny noshon

An dese days we always pan
haliday at her majesstees
xpense wid noff time fe grow
hare an resentment an vocabulary
fe cuss like caliban wid a girlee
magazine unda we pillow tick enoff
fe muffle we likkle nitely cry

Fe somwan we wooda call crappo
outside or som ringting call freedom
sweet like we seed dat a fall fallow
dat always comin down in seedy
places far de cast a bread
an is cole it cole like snow
hatin it we hate we self

So lay a bet pan de harses
hope fe a brake before yu back
bruk wid overtime enoff fe move
yu miserable backtoback sleep
to de wuk floor cause yu a sweat
like jackass but yu cawn see
de jackey wid blinka pan yu eye

Who gon deny yu yu half
battle a spirit who gon deny
a tirsty mule wata or a empty
engin ail wen dem a sit
in de saddle or behine
de weel cause dem cawn
drive wha nah wuk nar willin

So trow yu head back an droun
yu cares curl-up in a carna
an wet yu pants wake to a wirl
splittin de atom wid evry move
a yu head wish yu self dead
dan dis load yu a carry as lang
as yu rememba to noware fe notin

Town-Daddy

For Donald D'Aguiar

Friday afternoons the national bus from Georgetown,
Pulls up alongside the bridge at the front of the house
And is overtaken by sand, rain-cloud heading further inland.

We are there to greet it, one hand waves, one shades the eyes,
Edging right back from the road as it draws near,
Until we are perched on the parched lips of the trench.

Town-daddy in sandals with their fat leather strips
Criss-crossing, steps down as if testing the coolness of water,
The firmness of ground he can call his as far as sight.

He brings enough parcels for everyone to carry something,
Our neat O keeps swing-room for his walking-stick.
His sandal creaks as his heel rises and his weight pivots now

On the ball of one foot. There is the settling and unsettling
Of logs laid side by side as the entire calvacade cross
Into the yard's cricket-pitch path, left of the stunted guinep,

To the porch. Hear the bus pick-up, changing gears
Well into double figures as it mounts to the interior.
We lead him ducking through half-doors, three steps to mind.

What's always too soon is him making for the capital, so deep
Below sea-level that liners rear-up from the brimming water
Like fabulous ships of the air to land way in the sky.

Papa-T

For Reginald Messiah

When Grandad recited the Tennyson learned at sea,
I saw companies of redcoats tin-soldiering it
Through rugged country, picked off one by one
By poison-tipped blow-darts or arrows from nowhere:
Their drums panicky rattle, their bugler's yelp,
Musket-clap and popping cannons, smoke everywhere.

He'd cut short to shout, *If yu all don't pay me mind,*
I goin ge yu a good lickin an sen yu to bed, resuming
As he breathed in, his consonants stretched past recall,
Into a whales' crying place, beginning polyp kingdoms,
Shipwrecked into Amerindian care for months. We'd sit tight,
All eyes on our sweet seasalter, for that last-line-sound,

Someone mistimed once, making him start again.
These days the perfect-lined face of a blank page,
Startles at first, like Papa-T's no-nonsense recitals;
It has me itching to bring him reeling-off in that tongue –
Honor the charge they made! Honor the Light Brigade,
Noble six hundred: to hear, to disobey.

Ka-Tanx: a Prophesy

What brought him to the station?
The unpleasant part of our job,
Apologised the officer at the tail
Of a night-long, day-long procession,
Flooring us with what we knew deep-down.

On Christmas morning presents name us:
His are a quiet of being piled with balloons
Hardly releasing his breath, till day twelve.
We are as many months away from braving
The cupboard under stairs scaled by him;

Having to duck into the cool balaclava
Woven across it to what stands for him now –
His feet's leather, its heel worn to his walk.
For a stone pelted at him richocheted
Ka-tanx, as he dodged behind water-barrels,

His false-name since, and a prophesy:
The traveller who in a sidelong glance
Said, *He's too pretty by far to live long;*
Her hands cupped a charm from eyes
And wind alike, some blinding flame.

Masquerade

His passage of time is a series of dustclouds.
Streets widen at the end of town
Into sheer savannah, rolled bundles of bracken.

He watches a crow dip its beak and imagines
A living quill as its head throws back to swallow.

His cadillac is a well-kept secret
Plunged thirty feet to the bottom of this ravine.
The steering-wheel has him jacked to plush upholstery.

It's a B-road past disused miles of track
Running deep into exhausted mines.

As a child he skipped those sleepers
Or lay in wait for Black Boy, the daily steam-express
To flatten a six-inch nail into a knife.

It left a thick smoke trail that swept
Rice-paper-thin over ripening paddy.

It whistled at the crossroads where a woman
And child in a cart were carried
A quarter of a mile up the track.

He fished his brother out of a gully, found the mule
Grazing; his mother, no memory would want to account for.

Before a fit the skinned spider-monkeys
Failed to cure, he smells cut-grass and sees purple,
And a train, approaching his ear on the line.

The National Cycle Championship

By sun-up we'd lined the road,
Sporting psychedelic water-bottles
From Britain for Uncle,
Bound to pass leading the pack.

after an ages-wait
squeezed into a moment,
they rounded the bend,
bunched, head-down,
their tyres' million treads
pounding the red sand

We on tiptoes, necks craning
To make him out, imagined sandwiched
Amid the thick declensions
Of sparkling spokes, ridden for dear life.

few believed his hand
snatched the two I held:
plastic cords snapping,
my grip burned open –
one lost in spun yards
to catherine wheels

Deep that night he appeared,
Flat-out on the corrugated deck
Of a trailer, hugging the mangled
Thing, he'd made from scratch.

he wore a red coat,
save the saddle-print,
detailed as a tattoo
spanning his cleft,
U.S. sponsor
insignia an all

On Duty

Gun-metal is somehow cool even in this heat.
They press the cherished barrels to their cheeks
From time to time. Little else is done,
Nothing said, except to blow down the neck
Of uniforms or peer into the sight of a rifle.

It sharpens a wavering landscape under the nose,
And the capillaries of a browned, dust-caked leaf;
Including a man's lean, guarded figure, stepping clear
Of trees; whose bare soles seem to skip along
The steamy, bitumen-road, with hardly a touch.

It's a fragrance he loves, recalling days
When the giant Barber-Green unrolled its linoleum
Through the heart of this country.
It's a sight they have waited for all morning,
Beaten by this hottening monument hoisted now

To its zenith; rehearsing the features of this man,
Sure to come hot-stepping it to quench his thirst
At the official tap on the town's pipeline.
They have him lie face-down on the bonnet
Of a patrol car; it's a brand's warmth;

Its windscreen wipers poised on a dusty arc.
The engine's steady pulse drowns his own,
For it churrs and churrs, churning this memory
Like a broken record: how in broad daylight
They ordered three he knew to do press-ups

Till exhausted, then to run, barely able to break
Out of tottering before the guns blazed;
Giving his name as witness in the heat of it all,
And now this: a pistol to his head, they fire
An instruction, *Bwoy, we goin ge yu a chance, run!*

Out of this World

The path lay clean ahead,
Swanning up to me almost.
Where it dipped was fog
Mellowing a chain of streetlights
That looped-the-loop;
The farthest stationed like some East Star
I had to follow.

When I hit the basin of the valley,
It cooled from head to toe,
Fast enough to catch the mind;
Too soft to scare like a blow might.
I wouldn't know my twin at arm's length
In this; if the lamps outed
I'd have to feel my way home.

As I leaned into the hill,
It flashed how the run-down into here
Shoved and pulled at a walk-pace
I had a job keeping:
What's the point labouring against hard facts
When they clarify some notion I'd go red
To think face to face with another, much less say?

They'd use me as muscle to blunt the edges
Of everything: lamp posts, gradient, fog and all.
I'd come in for fuck-all save wind-bag praise
And a neat, neat epitaph,
Shat on by birds and moss alike.
People will stop scraping it with their soles
For its fuller sense.

Feeding the Ghosts

A solid absence, picturing the lost gold
Of El Dorado; the ruins of Great Zimbabwe.

A sudden shudder like the dive of mercury
Escaping a thermometer through minus.

The legs are the grassy brink of a precipice;
The kerosene-wick of a lamp kindles a volcano.

A tropical night, yet windows open wide,
Cannot draw any of a thousand insects in.

Generations of dust, in floorboard creases, stir.

Ol' Higue

She's blamed for our pulling back covers,
First thing, to a cold cabbage-doll,
Who bounced and gaw-gawed on our knees last night.

rain a fall, sun a shine
jumby a halla in-a bush

Tattered terracotta dress, on a lop-sided clothes-horse;
Merlin's cap or else a dunce's revealing the straw-head;
Be our plaything, or stay centred in a directionless field.

terracotta head, terracotta head
terracotta terracotta terracotta head

A trawler headed home, gulls trailing its wake:
Her porpoise-progress on the red sand road,
The tail of her dress sweeping it printless,
Her Gorgon's shoulder-glance at us pelting sand stones,
That explode round her spidery feet, and swing
Of the stick walking her, like a compass needle's
Freakish, instantaneous flight and return.

app-ten dapp-ten dee-kalapten
daddy kalapten dee-doo
eskamoo-dee skalam a-skoody
app-ten dapp-ten dee-kalapten
daddy kalapten dee-doo

Therefore she appears a low-flying comet,
Winds through keyholes with navigational ease,
Materialises beside a baby in its cot
All in sailor's blue and is drawn
To the brimming rice-bowl planted there.
She faces a compulsive's count,
Grain by polished grain till daybreak,
Deliberate waves of Kukumaka sticks
Converting her to bagged dominoes.

cushy cushy manae, cushy cushy manoe
bolo bolo masea, aikea jai jai jai

PART THREE Guyanese Days

Guyanese Days

As a child I worked this land half-naked,
Growing into patched, taken-in clothes.
It was one crop alongside another
For miles; tree-lined boundaries;
Paths wavering deep into shrubbery
Breaking onto clearings, far as the eye.

I used to sit and count the coconuts crash
Down: one this minute, two the next;
They skidded off branches, bounced trunks
To bang neat grooves in the mud, splash
Ponds or rolling, they'd come higgledy
Piggledy to nestle at my shaded spot.

Now I shake a Downs-tree bending ripe,
My head bent as its marble-sized fruits
Come showering in the first, huge drops
Of a downpour; my shirt held-up to load,
Eating a few choice ones in between;
Straightening to spit the seed far.

The balls of my feet dodge splintery
Plimplers as I pick up the dust track
Home, having to shoo the winged, stinging
Marabunta from my catch, tongue turning
A seed until smoothed white, humming
A tune that woke with me today.

Morning-school is a nursery rhyme
Sung till learned by heart, even tables,
So recall is an easy melody found whole;
This time Anancy tricks his wife and four
Children into each giving him half
Their share from a hard-won hand of bananas.

The pen was no fishing-rod made from a branch
Broken and shaped with a nail, my train-crushed
Knife, and dangled over fresh water, waiting
For the cork to dip, the worm still wriggling
On the zinc hook, its tip fanned to bite
Against pull, water creeping up the twine.

Once the bait took it dipped expanding circles.
The pen was harder to hold than the slingshot:
Limbs combed for the perfect fork, shaved
Of bark to gleam, two rubber bands strapped
Uppermost on the V and straddled by a tongue
For holding rounded, sun-baked clay.

The pen fought the push and pull of muscles:
Tsetse perched on a fence, my approach made
All afternoon, weight pivoted over the last
Inches, outstretched arm and the tail pincered
Between index finger and thumb, tied to string
And flown till boredom cut it loose or providence.

The blank page had no tale to tell:
What animal by its clover paw-print
Dared to cross the yard last night,
Losing itself once more to infinite
Pasture; where best to lay gum for birds
To light on and be caged; when rain.

Empty page gave eye-watering glare in sunshine.
Filling it – the nonsensical muddying of water
That squanders the gift of an afternoon swim;
Slingshot dropping short of ripest fruit.
Pen and page were like hoe and stony ground;
A full-moon smothered by reams of cloud.

The rhyme fell from my lips a thousand feet
Onto lined slate: coconut-husk stripped
On a half-sunken metal rod – such veined,
Bloodless flesh ripping with a hoarse cry;
Uprooting the shoots false-named 'growee'
For their sugary heart, mangroves were downed.

Left-handed, my knuckles whitened around the pen
Punctured the page, broke pencil-leads
Sharpened to stubbles running into miles
Of capital and common letters. Long before Z
I was sure it would come to zilch without teacher
To guide my hand, they slanted and buckled.

I dreamed through these afternoon exercises.
I'd find a shaded spot and see the way clouds
Form animals and demonic faces in blustering outlines.
They paraded my field of vision in a wind-blown
Trajectory of portraits and profiles. Anywhere
But facing the blackboard, flies warring

Among fine, stubborn, orbiting chalk-dust,
Wild cane swing hurtling it, the flies disbanded.
Or dodging my shadow: cast ahead one moment,
Following the next or lost under foot.
Grass tickling my in-step, I'd pull-up clumps
Between my clenched toes, the last stretch

To the shellpond dashed headlong,
The merest pause at the brink to kick-off
My khaki short-pants and a smarting belly-splash
That touched sand. The chalk-caked morning
Cleared with deep breaths, the rhythm of dive
After dive and the pen's zig-zag recedes, recedes.

Drag then the feet in small steps in silence
Back to newly thickening chalk-dust, to flies
Battling and teacher in front of class
In the same starched manner as if riveted
There all through lunch, flexing the cane
Into a bow or straight as an arrow with whistling flicks.

Pen and paper looked even glummer after noon.
They did teacher's every bidding like pets.
They felt like tools not held before,
Each letter a wringing of near-dry clothes,
Their joining a jolt of needle into finger;
Thimble-thoughts of the shell pond comforting.

Collected papers and pens stacked in airless,
Musty cupboards at the end of what seems like an age.
By now, chalk-dust solid in the sunbeams, the flies
Multiplied in the space above sir's desk and mine
Fast become a graveyard of row upon row
Facing their single, dustered headstone.

The run home: terylene unbuttoned
Shirt-tail flying in a cooler breeze
And the paling fence I had to slip sideways
Through after working one loose stave up
To double the gap, headfirst then the rest
Follows easily, left straight as a sentry.

For I am about the yard in search of parts:
A truck from two cans halved by twisting,
Made wheels, with a stick long as my leg
Nailed to a string-steered axle that broke
Out of control when we raced invisible circuits
Raising dust till the cricket and cicada cried dusk.

Or tractor from an empty spool, each tooth
Of its threaded wheels cut one by one in its edges.
It climbed everywhere powered by a wound rubber band
On a lever pulled between a pierced piece of candle.
Or a game of hop-scotch: squares drawn on ground
Pitch-clean, a dry mango seed for kicking,

Thrown and retrieved by hopping on one foot
Throughout. There'd be cheers and boos,
The index finger whipped against middle finger
And thumb, and the long, astonished whistle
At the accurate jab, the return hop heavy,
Burning; over the start-line was earth scaled.

Dusk's half-light thickening into pitch-night,
Batting till the boundary closed to the crease
Almost, flanked by house and road, having to stroke
The wooden ball under the verandah for four, fielding
On my stomach there; six if the palings cleared;
Always lashing out for runs, fast; or making a catch.

A half-calabash used to scoop water
Fetched in a bucket for a wash, the last of it
Poured by anyone nearby, the breeze goose-pimpling.
A buttonless shirt, knotted; a baggy trouser pinned;
The day's one cooked meal downed, grouped round
The gas lamp I so loved to pump, bright.

The calabash lived green and soft, its brain-grey
Insides scraped; it dried to a stiff, malleable
Gourd, perfect for years in the mud-oven kitchen
Where enamel flaked, iron dented, copper stained,
The hand-print wore away like the floorboards;
Then cracking like the bones of a septuagenarian.

The full moon rose and a million stars . . .
All gathered to watch how its lustre creams the sky
And is sometimes lost to cloud; all begged my fisted,
Frustrated hand 'say'. I took pen between middle
And index fingers as always, page at a slant.
The moon ducked clear of clouds into this vast opening

A shooting star's exact brightness shedded everywhere;
Across two hundred yards of pasture the shell pond's
Wind-pleated water for who could skip flat stones
The most; the tang of tamarind in the air, on the tongue;
That country under the moon's phosphorescence
Was vacant papyrus, my defining sight, its calligraphy.